MASTER
Your Thoughts

The Uninvited Mental Guests

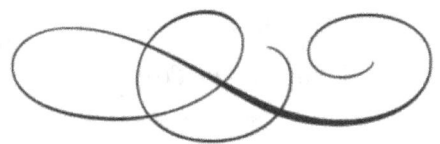

Harrison S. Mungal, Ph.D, Psy.D

Master Your Thoughts

Contact author via email: info@harrisonmungal.com
info@agetoage.ca
www.agetoage.ca
www.harrisonmungal.com
www.harrisonmungalbooks.com
Facebook: Harrison Mungal
Twitter: AgeToAgeInc1
LinkedIn: Harrison Mungal, Ph.D., PsyD
YouTube: Harrison Mungal
Phone: 905-533-1334

ABOUT *the*
AUTHOR

Harrison Sharma Mungal, BTh, MCC, MSW, PhD, PsyD

Harrison Sharma Mungal, possessing dual doctoral distinctions in Clinical Psychology and Philosophy in Social Work, demonstrates an unwavering commitment to ameliorating the well-being of his clients. Renowned internationally for his profound insights into cognitive therapy, his expertise spans mental health, addiction, relationships, and family dynamics.

In his role as a highly sought-after workshop presenter, Dr. Mungal extends his practical approach to assisting individuals, couples, families, and corporations. His global influence is evident through engaging presentations at conferences, seminars, and media platforms, where he adeptly integrates humor and enthusiasm into nuanced discussions on mental health, addiction, relationships, and parenting.

Dr. Mungal's innovative and scientifically grounded methodology has garnered acclaim, earning him accolades from diverse institutions. He extends his influence through offering training and consultations to a wide array of community partners, including esteemed professionals in the medical, social work, first responder, law enforcement, and senior management domains.

Actively involved in pioneering cognitive research, Dr. Mungal leads ground-breaking studies addressing mental health challenges such as addiction, psychosis, anxiety, and depression. His work includes the exploration of practical applications, exemplified by initiatives like music therapy for schizophrenia, substance abuse and addictions in the food service industry, and vaccination protocols for young children.

With over two decades of professional acumen, Dr. Mungal has left an indelible mark on the fields of mental health and psychiatry, providing services to diverse communities impacted by brain injuries, refugees, victims of warfare, and individuals in crisis. His pragmatic therapeutic repertoire encompasses evidence-based treatments like Cognitive Behavioural Therapy (CBT), Cognitive Processing Therapy (CPT), Dialectical Behavioural Therapy (DBT), Thought Developmental Practice (TDP) and Acceptance and Commitment Therapy (ACT).

TABLE *of* CONTENT

INTRODUCTION

This booklet contains excerpts from other books. It focuses only on the main topic as the title to help bring clarity and a better understanding to the reader. It covers more in-depth knowledge of the topic, specifically addressing self-destructive, intrusive, and impulsive thoughts. By mastering your thoughts, you can gain control over your mental landscape and live a more fulfilling life.

You will learn about self-destructive thoughts, and how they can be incredibly harmful, undermining our self-esteem and hindering our progress. They often stem from deep-rooted beliefs of unworthiness or inadequacy. Recognizing these thoughts is the first step towards mastering them. By challenging their validity and reframing them with more empowering beliefs, we can begin to break free from their grip.

You will learn about intrusive thoughts and how they can be relentless, barging into our minds without warning and causing distress. They may take the form of irrational fears or disturbing images. However, it's essential to understand that having intrusive thoughts doesn't make us abnormal or dangerous. Learning to observe these thoughts without judgment and letting them pass can help diminish their power over us. By practicing mindfulness and focusing on the present moment, we can learn to coexist with intrusive thoughts without allowing them to control us.

Impulsive thoughts often arise from a desire for instant gratification or a lack of impulse control. They can lead us to make hasty decisions or engage in reckless behaviors. To master impulsive thoughts, it's crucial to cultivate self-awareness and impulse control. By pausing to assess the consequences of our actions and considering alternative responses, we can learn to make more thoughtful choices. Developing healthy coping mechanisms, such as deep breathing or redirecting our focus, can also help curb impulsive tendencies.

Your will learn about cognitive restructuring and how it is a powerful technique for mastering your thoughts. It involves identifying and challenging negative thought patterns and replacing them with more realistic and positive alternatives. By recognizing the underlying beliefs driving our thoughts and reframing them in a more constructive light, we can change the way we perceive ourselves and the world around us. Through consistent practice, cognitive restructuring can help break the cycle of self-destructive, intrusive, and impulsive thinking.

Mindfulness practices play a crucial role in mastering your thoughts. By cultivating present-moment awareness, we can observe our thoughts without becoming entangled in them. Mindfulness techniques such as meditation, deep breathing, and body scans help quiet the mind and create space between our thoughts and our reactions. Over time, mindfulness empowers us to respond to our thoughts with greater clarity and intentionality, rather than reacting impulsively or succumbing to self-destructive patterns.

Mastering your thoughts is not always easy, and it's okay to seek support and guidance along the way. Therapy, support groups, or trusted friends and family members can provide valuable insight and encouragement. Surrounding yourself with positive influences and seeking professional help when needed can make the journey towards mastering your thoughts feel less daunting and more manageable.

"Master Your Thoughts" is a guide to overcoming self-destructive, intrusive, and impulsive thinking. It offers practical strategies for taking control of your mental well-being. By recognizing the destructive nature of self-destructive thoughts, confronting the intrusiveness of intrusive thoughts, and managing the impulsivity of impulsive thoughts, you can gain mastery over your mind. Through cognitive restructuring, mindfulness practices, and seeking support when needed, you can cultivate a more positive and empowering mental landscape. Remember, mastering your thoughts is a journey, not a destination. It requires patience, perseverance, and self-compassion. But by committing to the process, you can transform your relationship with your thoughts and live a life guided by intentionality and authenticity.

BREAK self-destructive
THOUGHTS

This chapter looks at harmful thinking patterns that can trap us and leave us stuck with dark thoughts. It is important to understand this issue because these thoughts impact more than just moods. They influence actions, relationships, and overall wellness. This chapter will identify harmful thought patterns, look closely at behaviours that continue them, and give useful strategies to break free. Whether the thoughts show up as constant self-pity, self-centeredness, or acting out for attention, recognizing them is the first move toward reclaiming mental freedom.

Unhelpful thinking patterns can steer us in the wrong direction. These thoughts make us do things, decide things, or feel things that are not good for us. They might pop up now and then or be deep habits that color how we see the world and ourselves. These thoughts come in many forms - doubting ourselves, feeling defeated, or expecting the worst, to name a few. Each one can negatively impact different parts of our lives, from self-esteem to relationships and careers.

The sneaky thing about these thoughts is how they feed themselves. For example, the thought "I'm not good enough" could stop you from applying for a job. Then you end up unemployed, which seems to prove the original thought right.

It's important to understand unhelpful thoughts because they often open the door to harmful actions and consequences. They act like distorted lenses that make everything seem to confirm their misleading story. To break this cycle, we first need to identify these thoughts for what they are: distortions, not truths. Once we spot them, we're in a better place to challenge and counteract them. We can use strategies like reframing our thinking or mindfulness to reshape our thought patterns in a more constructive way.

These distorted thoughts can sneak up on us. Left unchecked, they cause us to view ourselves and the world through a negative, hopeless lens. We see failure as certain and progress as impossible. In this mindset, we are prone to act in self-limiting or even self-destructive ways that align with the harmful stories we tell ourselves.

The first step is noticing when these thought patterns arise. Instead of automatically believing them, ask yourself: Is this thought helpful? Is it absolutely true? Or is it a distortion? What would be a more balanced, truthful viewpoint?

Once you identify the twisted thinking at play, you can start untwisting it. For example, replace broad labels like "I'm a failure" with specifics like "I failed at this particular task." Notice catastrophizing thoughts and replace them with calmer, more measured perspectives.

With practice, we can catch and reshape unhelpful thoughts before they send us down the wrong path. The more we challenge our distorted narratives, the less power they have over us. We can reclaim a clear-eyed view of ourselves and the world, acting with self-compassion instead of self-destruction.

Feeling constant self-pity keeps us stuck in negative thinking. While self-pity may temporarily make us feel better, it usually keeps us focused on the bad things. Over time, always thinking about our problems make us feel like a victim. We start to blame other people or things for our troubles and forget that we can take action. This makes a loop where not taking action leads to no progress, which confirms our thought that life is against us.

To break out of this harmful mindset, we need to challenge the urge to feel sorry for ourselves. We can do this by looking at the facts for and against our thoughts, identifying exaggerated thinking, and shifting our focus to solving problems. As we change from a victim mentality to a problem-solving view, we empower ourselves and undermine the basis of self-destructive thoughts.

Breaking free of self-destructive thoughts is about changing our life path, improving our mental health, and reaching our full potential. This chapter is a guide to help us identify, face, and dismantle these harmful thought patterns. This allows us to steer our lives in a more positive and fulfilling way.

Narcissistic personality traits can feed self-destructive thoughts. Narcissism may seem like too much self-love. But it often comes from deep self-doubt and insecurity. This leads to a fragile self-image that needs ongoing praise.

People with narcissistic traits constantly seek affirmation and attention. Their self-worth depends on others' approval. When approval is lacking, self-destructive thoughts can take over. Feelings of unworthiness, self-hate, and anger follow.

When a person feels very self-important and craves constant praise and admiration. Narcissists may believe they are extra special and deserve special treatment. When they don't get the constant validation they want, they feel hurt and lash out.

To change narcissistic patterns, it helps to develop more empathy. Understanding that others have needs too, not just you, is key. Also, find ways to feel good that don't depend on others' opinions. Focus on your own values and take pride in your real accomplishments. Don't just seek praise - do meaningful things.

Build a balanced, inner sense of self-worth. Don't rely on external praise or attention. With self-insight, narcissistic thought cycles are easier to stop. This prevents them from becoming self-destructive actions.

Another mental framework that can generate and maintain self-harming thoughts is borderline personality disorder (BPD).

Although not everyone who has self-destructive thoughts has BPD, grasping the condition provides critical insights into how emotional instability and black-and-white thinking can nourish destructive mental cycles. People with borderline tendencies often go through intense emotional swings and may find it hard to maintain a stable sense of identity. Their thoughts can rapidly oscillate between extremes, like idealization and criticism, making it tough to have a steady and constructive inner conversation.

Learning to manage emotions and thoughts effectively is vital in breaking the chain of self-harming thinking. Using a balanced approach to emotional experiences, rather than jumping to extremes, can significantly decrease the frequency and intensity of self-destructive thoughts. This prevents them from becoming self-destructive actions.

Borderline thinking can be very black-and-white. People are either perfect or terrible, with nothing in between. Moods swing rapidly between idealizing and hating the same person. Fears of abandonment are intense.

To break this cycle, try to see shades of gray. People are complex combinations of good and bad qualities. Moods naturally shift sometimes too. Practice radical acceptance - allowing life's ups and downs without exaggerating their meaning. Stay grounded in the present moment.

Sometimes, people think in ways that are harmful to themselves. These self-destructive thoughts can take different forms. Let's explore some common types of self-destructive thinking and how people can move past them.

Attention-seeking can lead to self-destructive thoughts. When craving attention gets extreme, failure to get it can spiral into very negative thinking. This often links to underlying issues like low self-worth.

Build a solid sense of self-esteem to avoid attention-seeking traps. Identify your values and real skills. Celebrate achievements that don't depend on others' views. Practice self-compassion. Set reasonable goals and work towards them. This lasting self-confidence makes outside attention less necessary.

Many types of unhealthy thinking patterns exist. We need to make positive changes tailored to each issue we struggle with. Develop empathy and self-love. See life's shades of gray. Find internal validation. With self-insight and the right tools, anyone can dismantle attention-seeking thinking habits and build more constructive thought patterns. The result is greater mental health and more power to direct your life in positive ways.

Making choices shapes how we think. Each choice we make - or avoid making - sends ripples through our future actions and thoughts. For example, deciding to tackle a tough problem might first make us anxious or scared. But it can eventually lead to feelings of strength and higher self-esteem. On the other hand, dodging challenges or taking the easy way out can reinforce thoughts that we're not good enough or have no power.

Making conscious choices takes knowing ourselves. This self-awareness often comes through reflective practices like journaling, meditation, or therapy. It also means weighing how choices will impact us not just right away, but in the long run. Being proactive in making choices that match our goals and values can greatly reduce negative thoughts. It can also nurture a more positive mindset.

While outside situations do shape our options, we have personal responsibility in directing our thinking. Admitting we're accountable for our choices is the first step toward changing future decisions and their effects on our thoughts. Taking responsibility flips us from a passive mindset, which can feed destructive thoughts, to an active one. This active stance is essential for constructive change.

Accountability should not be a platform for self-blame. Rather, it empowers us. It gives us control to shift behaviours and thought patterns. Reframing techniques can help us see poor choices or mistakes as chances to learn and grow. This transforms thoughts of regret into thoughts of opportunity.

Owning our choices requires courage and humility. But the personal growth and self-knowledge gained are invaluable. We can build emotional resilience when we reflect on choices candidly yet compassionately. This process reveals our core values and motivations. It also uncovers unconscious biases we may hold.

With time and practice, we can become more adept at making choices aligned with our best self. The better we know ourselves, the better we can anticipate whether a choice will lead to constructive or destructive thought patterns. We can catch and reshape negative thinking before it takes hold.

No one is perfect. There will always be choices we later wish we could change. Self-judgment only repeats old thought loops. Instead, we can focus on the insights gained for making wiser choices moving forward. We can also extend the same gentle understanding to others making difficult choices.

In this way, conscious choice-making creates a upwards spiral. As we become more mindful of our thought patterns, we can steadily shift our thinking in a positive direction. The more constructively we think, the better choices we tend to make. Our choices then reinforce and reflect our personal growth.

Apologizing and forgiving can have big effects on how we think. Saying "I'm sorry" in a real way can free your mind from feelings of guilt or regret. Forgiving someone can help stop thoughts of anger or wanting to get even. Even when you know you are right, choosing to say sorry can reduce tension, inside yourself and with others. It can open the door to more helpful thoughts.

Similarly, forgiveness does not say the other person was right. But it frees us from carrying around negative feelings. It cleans out our emotions in a way. This makes room for more positive, constructive thinking. Things like empathy training can make it easier to forgive. Forgiving reduces stress and improves mental health a lot.

Saying "I'm sorry" can also be a tool to manage negative thoughts. It can mark the moment we realize our thinking has become negative or self-destructive. It signals it's time to switch to a more constructive way of thinking, by acknowledging the negative thought and committing to changing that thought pattern going forward.

The capacity to apologize and forgive are important emotional skills. Saying "I'm sorry" sincerely can free your mind from guilt. Forgiving cleanses negative emotions to make way for positivity. Apologizing reduces tension and opens the door to constructive thoughts. Forgiving decreases stress and improves well-being.

Apologizing marks negative thoughts, signaling it's time to change thinking. Forgiving declutters emotions to clear space for growth. Together they transform thinking in a multi-step process. It takes self-awareness, responsible choices, and emotional intelligence. When understood deeply, apologizing and forgiving build a framework for dismantling destructive thoughts. This understanding enables nourishing new mental landscapes to emerge.

Saying "I'm sorry" and "I forgive you" are powerful phrases. They can rewrite mental patterns that limit us. Apology liberates, reducing inner turmoil. Forgiveness cleanses, inviting spaces for renewal. Both require courage and vulnerability. Their transformative potential is unlocked through empathy. With compassion, they become tools to recalibrate the mind. Wielded with care, they can cultivate thinking anew.

These small phrases unlock tremendous inner power. Apology liberates us from the past's weight. Forgiveness lifts the heart's heaviness. Together they allow new choices, new space. With courage, we unlock their potential for growth. When we apologize and forgive authentically, we transform. Our minds become free to create, connect, and nourish. We cultivate new landscapes of thought.

INTRUSIVE THOUGHTS the uninvited MENTAL GUESTS

Our minds are complex and mysterious. Sometimes thoughts pop into our heads that are troubling and seem to come out of nowhere. These kinds of thoughts are called intrusive thoughts. Intrusive thoughts can make people feel distressed, scared or upset. Even though we might like to think we have complete control over our own minds, intrusive thoughts show that's not always true.

Intrusive thoughts are thoughts that seem to burst into our minds without us wanting them there. They arrive without invitation and overstay their welcome, leaving us puzzled and troubled. We did not consciously choose to think these thoughts, yet there they are inside our heads. Sometimes they are fleeting, but other times they stubbornly stick around against our wishes.

We wonder, "Where did that thought come from?" and "Why can't I make it go away?"

These unwelcome mental intruders disrupt our peace of mind. When we are going about our daily lives, focusing on work or connecting with loved ones, intrusive thoughts rudely barge in unannounced. They distract us and evoke unpleasant emotions like fear, disgust or doubt. We may feel ashamed of having such strange thoughts and try to push them out of awareness. However, suppressing intrusive thoughts often backfires by making them return stronger.

Though intrusive thoughts cause distress, they are a common and normal human experience. Most people have them at some point. They do not mean someone is flawed or crazy. However, when intrusive thoughts are very frequent or upsetting, professional help may be warranted. Cognitive behavioral therapy is effective for managing intrusive thoughts that severely impact daily functioning.

Understanding where intrusive thoughts come from is the first step to managing them. These thoughts barge in like rude guests, surprising you and messing up your mind. They come from many places - bad experiences like failing at something or getting your heart broken, hurtful words or criticism from others, or emotional and psychological scars from past traumas that still affect you. The random, sudden way these thoughts pop up can be especially upsetting. They interrupt your normal thinking, distract you, and can make you feel bad emotionally. So it's really important to understand where they come from, not just to satisfy curiosity but to actually help yourself cope with them. Their origins could be buried deep in your personal history, lying dormant for years before something happening now triggers them.

Intrusive thoughts are like weeds popping up out of nowhere in a garden you've tended with care. You need to figure out where they came from to properly pull them out by the roots. Did they grow from seeds blown in unpredictably by the wind, meaning they arose spontaneously with no clear cause? Or did they sprout from seeds laid long ago that now, under certain conditions, have decided to germinate?

In either case, learning the source of intrusive thoughts takes some gardening know-how and diligent inspection of the soil. Kneel down, dig around the base of the weed, and trace its roots as far down as you can go. Examine the texture of the soil, notice rocks or hardened clay that may have blocked the roots from going deeper. Keep exploring gently but persistently, even if the roots twist out of sight.

Getting to the absolute bottom of the roots is often impossible. But uncovering even a portion of them can help you understand the conditions that allowed this weed to grow. Does the soil contain contaminants from past fertilizers that have destabilized the ecosystem? Is there a shallow layer of topsoil that encourages surface-level rooting? Are essential nutrients depleted in certain areas?

Your discoveries will inform the strategies you use to restore balance and order. Pulling the weed is just the first step. You'll also need to improve the soil, plant intentionally, and nourish the good seeds that will grow into a healthy garden. It's hard work, but the reward is a vibrant landscape you tend with care and joy.

The same is true in managing intrusive thoughts. Identifying where they came from, as best you can, gives you power over them. You realize the conditions that allowed them to take root, so you can start changing those conditions. It's a process - but like weeding a garden, the work you put in over seasons will make all the difference.

Making choices is a big part of our lives. Some of our choices don't matter much, like picking what to wear or eat. But other choices can change our lives forever. Having the freedom to choose for ourselves is great. But it also means we have to take responsibility for what happens after we choose. Nobody is perfect. We all make mistakes sometimes and choose wrong. Those mistakes can stay with us, making us feel bad long after they happen.

When our choices turn out bad, or we realize we chose wrong, it can really bother us. The memories of those mistakes keep popping back up in our heads. We can't stop thinking about what we did wrong, and how we wish we did things differently. These thoughts that keep coming back can make us feel down on ourselves. They can even make it hard to make more choices, because we're afraid we'll just mess up again. Stuck in the past, the mistakes make it tough to grow and feel good about ourselves now.

If we can step back and see those stuck thoughts for what they are - echoes of past mistakes, not signs we're bad people - it helps. Beating ourselves up over and over about a wrong choice we can't take back just makes us miserable. Those thoughts try to trick us into believing we're worthless because of some errors. But mistakes don't define anyone's true value or potential.

In our brains, those recurring thoughts about regrets are out of place, like weeds in a garden. They don't belong, because they don't help us live our best lives in the present. We have to understand where the thoughts come from to pull them out by the roots. If we can connect them to the specific choices and times in our lives when we felt regret, it gets easier to handle them. Armed with that insight, we can start to take away their power over us.

Unwelcome thoughts are not random, they show up for a reason. Knowing that reason helps us address what's really bothering us instead of just feeling bad. Pulling up those mental weeds, and focusing our energy on growing new, positive thoughts is the best way forward. When we can push past the mistakes and see our true value, we take back control. Our minds become peaceful gardens again, where our self-esteem and potential can blossom.

The way we grow up affects how we think and learn. Families shape children's emotional and thinking skills. From the time we're little to when we're teens, our home life builds our foundation. If kids don't get what they need, it can cause problems that last. Hurtful homes can lead to recurring thoughts that bother us. These thoughts echo the unstable places we grew up in. They follow us into adulthood and affect us in many ways.

For example, a child whose family only showed love when they behaved may struggle with thoughts about being worthy and lovable. Or a child who was often criticized or humiliated may battle self-doubt or extreme shyness as an adult. Because families are often the first social structure kids know, what we learn there sticks with us. It can be very hard to change. Seeing recurring thoughts as leftovers from a rocky childhood can help people identify why they struggle with thinking. This allows them to get the right psychological help.

The family environment shapes the way we see ourselves and the world. Warm, stable homes help children feel safe and valued. This gives them a solid base to build thinking skills. But hurtful, unstable homes have lasting effects. They undermine children's sense of security and self-worth. This leads to recurring negative thoughts that don't match reality. For instance, someone neglected as a child may struggle as an adult to see their worth. Even loving relationships may not ease their self-doubt.

There is a powerful tie between upbringing and cognitive health. Our thought patterns and coping strategies originate early in life. A child who couldn't depend on parents may become an anxious adult who expects rejection. An adult still haunted by childhood emotional abuse may battle low self-esteem. Even small daily stresses may echo old wounds.

The great news is that we can heal from our upbringing's effects with time and care. Counseling helps us understand where intrusive thoughts come from, building new social connections allows healthy relating skills to develop, and self-compassion helps counter old shame. There are many effective ways to rewrite old cognitive patterns.

While we can't change the past, we can change how we relate to it. Recognizing the root of intrusive thoughts helps decrease their power over us. They become understandable responses rather than unexplained burdens. This clarity guides us toward helpful solutions tailored to our unique life story. With care and courage, we can build new cognitive frameworks that support our health and dreams. Our upbringing shapes but does not define us. There is hope for all who seek it.

Traumatic events can leave lasting marks on a our minds. These events can set the stage for intrusive thoughts that might continue for many years, possibly a whole lifetime. The sneaky nature of trauma-related intrusive thoughts is that they can pop up suddenly. They are set off by things that may seem unrelated or harmless. Trauma fundamentally changes how the brain handles information and responds to stress. It often makes the brain overly sensitive to triggers that can set off a rush of intrusive thoughts.

For example, someone who survived a car accident might experience intrusive thoughts when they hear the sound of screeching tires. Or someone who went through emotional abuse may feel overwhelmed by thoughts of not being good enough when faced with criticism. To make matters worse, the thoughts themselves can become triggers for more emotional and physical reactions. Like anxiety attacks. This creates a vicious cycle that is hard to break.

There are also many self-care habits that can aid trauma recovery and resilience. Getting enough sleep, eating healthy foods, exercising, and avoiding drugs and alcohol are all important. So are practices like meditation, journaling, spending time in nature, and doing enjoyable activities. Maintaining strong social support and asking for professional help when needed are also key.

Healing from trauma takes time. The road is different for everyone. But with the right support, tools, and determination, we can learn to manage intrusive thoughts. The thoughts may never fully go away. However, their disruptive power can be greatly reduced. This makes room for more peace and presence in daily life.

Intrusive thoughts are unwelcome ideas that seem to come from out of nowhere. They invade our minds when we least expect them. These troubling thoughts can make us feel ashamed, guilty, or afraid. Experts say intrusive thoughts are common. Most people have them at some point. But when intrusive thoughts happen a lot, they can really bother us.

Intrusive thoughts cause problems because they make us blame ourselves. Our minds can be very good at making us feel responsible, even for things that weren't our fault. Intrusive thoughts that come from misplaced blame are extra troubling. They create a false story about why the thought happened.

For example, someone bullied as a child might have intrusive thoughts that the abuse was their own fault. Their mind tells them they deserved it because of who they are. This distorted thinking can stick with them as a core belief. It colours how they see themselves in every situation after that. But the truth is they were innocent. The bullying was not their fault, no matter what their thoughts tell them. Realizing they are blaming themselves for no good reason is an important step. It helps them see the intrusive thoughts are lies, not truth.

Therapy focused on self-compassion can help. It teaches them not to believe the distorted ideas the intrusive thoughts create. Reminding themselves they did not deserve the bullying replaces false blame with true understanding.

Looking into what causes intrusive thoughts is useful too. A troubled childhood, trauma, or deep shame can all play a role. When we understand where intrusive thoughts come from, we can weaken their power over us. We can use therapy techniques targeted at their roots. This helps us handle intrusive thoughts in healthier ways.

The path to reclaiming peace of mind is not easy when intrusive thoughts have built false beliefs over time. But by facing their origins, we can unravel their hold on our emotional health. We can rewrite the false narratives they have created. With compassion, truth, and the right tools, we can find freedom from intrusive thoughts' harsh judgments. Our minds become calmer, clearer, and more focused on the present. We regain control of our thoughts and can live with self-acceptance.

The first step is recognizing that blame from intrusive thoughts is misplaced. This helps us take back power over our beliefs. Our thoughts can go from disturbing to quiet, from negative to neutral. In time we find clarity, perhaps for the first time in a long time. By easing suffering caused by intrusive thoughts, we ease our suffering as whole people. We end their unwarranted blame and change our relationship with ourselves.

Our thoughts can be sorted into different groups based on how intentional they are and how much they impact what we do. Some thoughts just drift through our minds without having an immediate effect. These are passive thoughts. They might be as simple as remembering what you ate for breakfast or as complicated as thinking about the meaning of life in general. Other thoughts are on purpose and aimed at reaching specific goals. These planned thoughts are things like making a schedule for your day or figuring out a problem. Active thoughts lead directly to taking action right away. These thoughts guide our behavior and choices we make.

The relationship between these kinds of thoughts and intrusive thoughts can be tricky. Passive thoughts can turn into intrusive thoughts when they are unwanted and get in the way. They sidetrack planned or active thoughts. For example, while getting ready to give a big presentation at work, intrusive thoughts about a recent breakup could break your focus and keep you from being as productive. Recognizing the type and nature of each thought can help people better control their thinking. Strategies that affect thinking can turn disruptive passive thoughts into planned or active thoughts that are helpful instead of harmful.

Rather than letting our minds wander wherever they want, it is helpful to take charge of our thoughts and guide them in productive directions. With practice, we can learn to minimize time spent on passive thoughts that have no purpose. We can also catch intrusive thoughts and turn our attention to more positive planned and active thoughts. This allows us to focus mental energy on achieving goals that are important to us.

A useful step is to become more aware of when our thoughts start to drift into passive or intrusive territory. Sometimes this happens without us even noticing at first. Checking in with ourselves regularly to monitor our thought patterns is important. When we tune into our thoughts, we can consciously decide how to respond to them. Rather than letting passive or intrusive thoughts take over, we can deliberately shift our focus.

We have power over our inner world of thoughts and don't have to let unhelpful thinking run wild. It simply takes commitment to exercise this mental muscle. With time, we can cultivate control over thoughts that once felt out of our control. Monitoring, evaluating and redirecting thoughts becomes easier. Progress won't happen overnight, but as we practice these skills our mental discipline will grow.

This process allows us to take an active role over our inner experience. We can move toward a place where our thoughts align with and support our goals and values. Rather than being controlled by passive and intrusive thoughts, we become equipped to intentionally craft thoughts that contribute to the life we want to build. Our thinking patterns can go from holding us back to propelling us forward.

People often remember bad experiences more clearly than good ones. This tendency has been linked to evolutionary psychology - our ancient survival instincts. Focusing on the negative helped early humans notice dangers and threats. But in the modern world, where most dangers are less immediate, this negativity bias can be harmful.

The bias shows up in intrusive thoughts as "negative memory cards." These are distressing thoughts that repeat in the mind, like a skipping record. They often recall past mistakes, regrets, failures - any kind of perceived shortcoming. To replace the negative cards, we need to purposefully acknowledge and appreciate positive experiences.

One way is practicing mindfulness. This means paying close attention to the present moment. When we feel joy or accomplish something, mindfulness helps us fully take it in. We can capture these little wins as they happen. Over time, they counterbalance the negative thoughts.

We can also look back purposefully for successes to celebrate. Remembering past achievements and wins helps build more positive memory cards. The more we actively seek out positives from our life, the more our brain retains them.

Techniques like positive affirmations and gratitude journals are proven to rewire thinking. Affirmations are short phrases we repeat about our strengths and abilities. Saying them regularly combats negative self-talk. Gratitude journals help us regularly write down things we're thankful for. This builds up positive memories to draw on.

Dealing with the past can be tough. Sometimes the past just won't leave us alone. It keeps popping up in our thoughts and affecting what we do today. Those old memories and experiences are stored away in our minds like a big archive of files. When those files contain a lot of negative stuff, it weighs us down. It's like carrying around a heavy backpack everywhere you go. This extra weight makes it hard to think clearly and feel good.

So how can we "cancel the past" and feel freer emotionally and mentally? The first step is to open up those old memory files and take a fresh look. Are they still accurate? Are they still relevant to today? Getting help from a counselor or therapist can make this easier since old memories can be complex. They will work with you to reevaluate each past experience. Once you can see the past more clearly, its grip on the present will loosen.

Intrusive thoughts that pop up unwanted are also tangled up in our past experiences. These disruptive thoughts have roots in many places - our personal history, the way our brains work, the biases we've developed over time. To reduce intrusive thoughts, we need to trace back to the source and understand what's causing them. Helpful tools include therapy techniques, mindfulness practices, and purposefully changing our thought patterns. This takes effort but can make a big difference in reclaiming mental space.

In conclusion, the past does not have to define us. We can decrease its influence in the here and now. This takes courage to confront old memories, guidance to reassess them, and commitment to let them go. Though challenging, this work can free up our minds, improve emotional health, and allow us to live more fully in the present. With help and perseverance, we can break the grip of the past. We can refuse to allow old hurts or habits to weigh us down. Step by step, we can create space for clearer thinking and greater inner peace.

IMPULSIVE THOUGHTS

We need to embark on a journey of self-reflection and introspection, aiming to understand the nature of impulsive thoughts and uncover the underlying causes that give rise to them. Understanding the intriguing realm of impulsive thoughts and exploring how they can significantly impact our lives is essential. This will help us to "*Master Your Thoughts*" from abuse, traumas, addictions, toxic relationships, a negative past, regrets, mistakes, and wrongdoings.

Impulsive thoughts have a way of sneaking into our minds, often leading us to react without much consideration or deliberation. They can manifest in various forms, from spontaneous decisions to sudden bursts of anger or impetuous behaviours. These automatic reactions can have far-reaching consequences, affecting our relationships, mental well-being, and overall quality of life.

To effectively address impulsive thoughts, we must first recognize and identify them as they arise. By understanding the triggers that prompt these automatic reactions, we can gain greater awareness of our thoughts and emotions in the heat of the moment—furthermore, understanding our past experiences and how they can shape our impulsive thinking, shedding light on the roots of these patterns and their influence on our present mindset.

Emotions play a significant role in impulsive thoughts. They can act as powerful catalysts, intensifying our automatic reactions and clouding our judgment. By investigating the intricate relationship between emotions and impulsive thinking, we can gain valuable insights into navigating and managing these intense feelings more effectively.

Cognitive restructuring lies at the heart of this chapter, offering a powerful tool for reframing our automatic reactions. By subjecting our thoughts to logical examination, we can challenge their validity and consider alternative perspectives. We can aim to cultivate a more rational and balanced mindset through cognitive restructuring, enabling us to respond thoughtfully and purposefully to life's challenges.

We need to explore the importance of questioning assumptions and evaluating the validity of our automatic thoughts and beliefs. By actively seeking alternative interpretations and viewpoints, we open ourselves to broader possibilities, fostering greater flexibility and resilience in our thinking.

Ultimately, our goal should be to equip ourselves with problem-solving strategies rooted in critical thinking. By honing our ability to overcome impulsive thoughts, we can gain the tools to navigate life's twists and turns with clarity, wisdom, and emotional well-being.

We take a transformative journey together as we explore the world of impulsive thoughts, examining and reframing our automatic reactions. We need to take a hike through the landscapes of our minds as we navigate the path to emotional well-being.

Impulsive thoughts are spontaneous, rapid, and often involuntary mental responses that arise in various situations. These thoughts can be impulsive actions, judgments, or emotional reactions that occur without much forethought or reflection. They tend to arise automatically and can significantly impact our lives, influencing our behaviours, decision-making processes, and relationships.

One key characteristic of impulsive thoughts is their immediate nature. They often emerge swiftly without giving us much time to consider their consequences or evaluate their validity. These thoughts can manifest as impulsive actions, such as making impulsive purchases, engaging in risky behaviours, or saying something without thinking about its potential impact. They can also take the form of impulsive judgments, where we quickly form opinions about others or situations based on limited information or biases.

The impact of impulsive thoughts on our lives can be far-reaching. They can lead to regrettable actions, damaged relationships, and missed opportunities. When we act on impulsive thoughts without considering the potential consequences, we may find ourselves facing unfavourable outcomes or experiencing negative emotions such as guilt, shame, or disappointment.

Impulsive thoughts can also affect our decision-making processes. They often bypass rational thinking and logical analysis, leading us to make hasty or uninformed choices. This can be particularly problematic in situations that require careful consideration, such as financial decisions, career choices, or interpersonal conflicts.

Moreover, impulsive thoughts can influence our relationships with others. When we form quick judgments or react impulsively based on our automatic thoughts, we may misinterpret others' intentions, overlook their perspectives, or engage in conflict unnecessarily. This can lead to misunderstandings, strained relationships, and missed opportunities for empathy and understanding.

Understanding the nature and impact of impulsive thoughts is crucial for gaining control over them. By recognizing their spontaneous and automatic nature, we can develop strategies to challenge and reframe these thoughts. By exploring the influence of impulsive thoughts on our lives, we can become more aware of their potential drawbacks and seek ways to mitigate their negative impact.

To challenge and reframe our impulsive thoughts, it is crucial to first identify them and understand their triggers. Automatic reactions are thoughts and behaviours that arise automatically and without conscious effort. They often occur in response to specific situations, events, or stimuli and can significantly impact our lives if left unexamined.

Recognizing impulsive thoughts requires a heightened sense of self-awareness. It involves paying close attention to our internal dialogue and emotional responses in different situations. For example, imagine a scenario where you receive constructive criticism from a colleague, a friend or a family member. An impulsive thought in this situation might be, "They think I'm incompetent and don't value my work." This automatic reaction might be triggered by insecurity or a fear of failure.

It is helpful to pause and reflect on our immediate responses to various events to identify impulsive thoughts. This could involve keeping a journal or making mental notes of situations that elicit strong emotional reactions. By observing our thoughts and emotions without judgment, we can unravel the patterns of our automatic reactions.

Paying attention to physical cues accompanying impulsive thoughts is also essential. These cues can manifest as increased heart rate, tense muscles, or a sudden surge of adrenaline. Being attuned to these bodily sensations can serve as an indicator that impulsive thoughts are arising.

Triggers for impulsive thoughts can vary widely and are unique to each person. They can be linked to past experiences, fears, insecurities, or specific environments. For instance, someone who has experienced a traumatic event might have impulsive thoughts triggered by situations that resemble or remind them of that event. Triggers can be more subtle, such as specific words or phrases that evoke strong emotional reactions.

By identifying the triggers associated with our impulsive thoughts, we gain insight into our automatic reactions' underlying causes and patterns. This awareness allows us to effectively develop strategies to challenge and reframe these thoughts.

Impulsive reactions can often be traced to underlying causes influencing our thought processes and behaviours. By examining these roots, we gain a deeper understanding of why we react impulsively and can begin to address and manage these reactions more effectively.

One significant factor in impulsive reactions is our conditioning and learned behaviours. Throughout our lives, we acquire specific patterns of thinking and acting based on our experiences and the environments we grew up in. If we were raised in a strict and authoritarian household, we might have developed a tendency to react impulsively when faced with authority figures or rules. Similarly, if we witnessed impulsive behaviour being rewarded or praised in the past, we may have internalized those behaviours as acceptable or adequate.

Society often places expectations and pressures on us, and when we perceive a deviation from these norms, it can trigger impulsive responses. For instance, if we feel judged or criticized for not conforming to societal standards, we may react impulsively to defend ourselves or seek approval.

Moreover, our core beliefs and values can also influence impulsive reactions. These deep-rooted convictions shape our perception of the world and ourselves. If we hold rigid beliefs prioritizing immediate gratification or self-preservation above all else, we are more likely to engage in impulsive behaviour. These beliefs stem from personal experiences, cultural influences, or biological factors.

Furthermore, certain psychological factors can contribute to impulsive reactions. Conditions such as attention deficit hyperactivity disorder (ADHD) or borderline personality disorder (BPD) are characterized by impulsivity as a core symptom. These conditions may result from a combination of genetic, neurological, and environmental factors, making us more prone to impulsive thoughts and behaviours.

When examining the roots of impulsive reactions, it is essential to consider the role of our emotions. Emotions play a significant role in influencing our thoughts and actions. Intense emotions, including anger, fear, or excitement, can override our rational thinking processes, leading to impulsive behaviour. Understanding our emotional triggers and learning to regulate our emotions can help mitigate impulsive reactions.

Examining the roots of impulsive reactions involves exploring the interplay of various factors. Our conditioning, learned behaviours, social and cultural influences, core beliefs, psychological factors, and emotional responses contribute to impulsive thoughts and behaviours. By gaining insight into these underlying causes, we can develop strategies to manage and reframe our automatic reactions more effectively. Through self-reflection, therapy, and personal growth, we can gradually reduce the influence of impulsive thinking and make more deliberate and reasoned choices in our lives.

Our past experiences significantly shape our thoughts, behaviours, and reactions, including impulsive thinking. When examining impulsive thoughts, it becomes crucial to delve into our personal history and explore the events that may have influenced our automatic reactions.

Past experiences can create patterns of thinking that contribute to impulsive thoughts. If someone has experienced a series of adverse or traumatic events, they may develop a pessimistic outlook on life. This negative outlook can lead to impulsive thoughts, including assuming the worst in every situation or jumping to conclusions without considering alternative explanations.

Similarly, childhood experiences and upbringing can shape impulsive thinking. Those of us who grew up in an environment where our opinions were consistently dismissed or invalidated may develop impulsive thoughts of self-doubt or a constant need for validation from others. These thought patterns can impact decision-making processes, resulting in impulsive behaviours seeking immediate approval or validation.

Moreover, past failures or setbacks can also contribute to impulsive thinking. If someone has experienced repeated disappointments or rejections, they may develop a fear of failure or a sense of urgency to act quickly without considering the potential consequences. This fear can lead to impulsive thoughts, including taking unnecessary risks or making hasty decisions without careful deliberation.

Understanding how past events shape impulsive thinking allows us to gain insight into our automatic reactions. By identifying the specific experiences that have influenced our thought patterns, we can begin to challenge and reframe those thoughts more constructively.

One practical approach is to engage in reflective exercises or therapy that encourages exploring past events and their impact on current thought processes. This exploration can help us identify any negative or limiting beliefs that have emerged from their past experiences. Once these beliefs are recognized, we can work towards reframing them by seeking evidence to challenge their validity.

By examining and unpacking past experiences, we can better understand the root causes behind impulsive thoughts. This understanding provides a foundation for personal growth and allows us to develop more balanced and rational thinking patterns. It enables us to break free from the limitations imposed by past events. It empowers us to make more informed decisions based on the present circumstances rather than automatic reactions rooted in the past.

Cognitive restructuring is a powerful technique that helps us challenge and reframe our automatic reactions and impulsive thoughts through logical examination. It involves examining the underlying assumptions and beliefs contributing to impulsive thinking and replacing them with more rational and balanced alternatives. By engaging in cognitive restructuring, we can gain greater control over our thoughts and make more informed and constructive decisions.

Cognitive restructuring is awareness of the automatic reactions and impulsive thoughts that arise in various situations. This requires mindfulness and attentiveness to one's thinking patterns. We can identify the underlying beliefs and assumptions that drive our impulsive reactions by paying close attention to emerging thoughts.

Once these automatic thoughts and underlying beliefs are identified, the next step is critically examining their validity. This involves questioning the evidence supporting these thoughts and considering alternative explanations and perspectives. It is vital to challenge the accuracy and fairness of these thoughts and consider whether they are based on facts or distorted perceptions.

One effective technique in cognitive restructuring is called "evidence gathering." This involves systematically collecting evidence that supports or refutes automatic thoughts and beliefs. By evaluating this evidence's strength and reliability, we can better understand the accuracy of our initial reactions. This process helps to counteract cognitive biases and encourages a more balanced and objective assessment of the situation.

Additionally, we can use logical reasoning to reframe our automatic reactions. This involves identifying logical errors or cognitive distortions in our thinking, including overgeneralization, jumping to conclusions, or catastrophizing. By challenging these distorted thinking patterns, we can replace them with more realistic and rational thoughts.

It is essential to replace automatic reactions with alternative and more balanced thoughts. This can be achieved by generating alternative explanations or interpretations of the situation. We can broaden our understanding and develop more flexible thinking patterns by considering different perspectives. This process encourages us to consider the possibility of positive outcomes, potential solutions, or alternative ways of perceiving the situation.

Furthermore, cognitive restructuring involves practicing and reinforcing new rational thoughts. This requires repetition and consistency to strengthen the neural pathways associated with the revised thinking patterns. Over time, we can develop a habit of questioning our automatic reactions and replacing them with more reasoned and balanced thoughts.

Developing rational thinking is crucial in challenging impulsive thoughts and reframing automatic reactions. Impulsive thoughts often stem from distorted thinking patterns and cognitive biases that lead to irrational beliefs and actions. By cultivating a more rational and balanced mindset, we can gain greater control over our impulsive thoughts and make more informed decisions.

One of the critical aspects of developing rational thinking is learning to recognize and challenge cognitive distortions. Cognitive distortions are habitual patterns of thinking that skew our perception of reality. Cognitive distortions include black-and-white thinking (seeing things as either all good or all bad), overgeneralization (drawing broad conclusions based on limited evidence), and personalization (assuming excessive responsibility for events that are beyond our control). By becoming aware of these distortions, we can begin to question their validity and replace them with more accurate and balanced thoughts.

Cultivating rational thinking is learning to separate facts from interpretations and assumptions. Our minds often generate automatic thoughts based on limited information and personal biases. These thoughts can be highly subjective and may not align with objective reality. We can gain a more balanced perspective on a situation by critically examining the evidence and seeking alternative explanations. This involves asking ourselves questions like, "What evidence do I have to support this thought?" and "Are there other possible explanations for this situation?"

Developing rational thinking entails adopting a more flexible and open-minded attitude. It involves acknowledging that our initial perceptions and judgments may not always be accurate or complete. By actively seeking alternative perspectives and considering different viewpoints, we can broaden our understanding of a situation and challenge our impulsive thoughts more effectively. This can be achieved through techniques such as perspective-taking, where we attempt to put ourselves in someone else's shoes and see things from their point of view.

Furthermore, developing rational thinking involves honing critical thinking skills. This includes the ability to analyze information objectively, identify logical fallacies, and evaluate the reliability and validity of sources. By applying critical thinking, we can approach our impulsive thoughts with skepticism and examine them more logically and rationally. This process often involves asking questions like, "What evidence supports this thought?" and "Is this thought based on facts or assumptions?"

Ultimately, developing a more rational and balanced mindset requires practice and patience. It is a skill that can be cultivated through consistent effort and self-reflection. By challenging impulsive thoughts and reframing automatic reactions, we can gain greater control over our decision-making process and lead more fulfilling and meaningful lives.

In our daily lives, we often make assumptions and hold beliefs without consciously examining their validity. These automatic thoughts can contribute to impulsive reactions, as they may be based on limited information, biased perspectives, or past experiences that no longer hold.

When faced with impulsive thoughts or reactions, it is crucial to take a step back and examine the underlying assumptions that fuel them. Assumptions are often deeply ingrained in our thinking patterns and can influence our behaviour without realizing it. By questioning our assumptions, we can challenge their accuracy and uncover any cognitive distortions that may be present.

To begin questioning assumptions, it is helpful to identify the thoughts or beliefs driving our impulsive reactions. These thoughts may manifest as inner dialogue, self-talk, or mental images accompanying impulsive behaviour. Once we have identified these automatic thoughts, we can subject them to scrutiny.

One effective strategy for evaluating the validity of our automatic thoughts is to gather evidence both for and against them. This involves examining the facts and considering alternative explanations or interpretations of the situation. By engaging in this process, we can gain a more balanced perspective and reduce the influence of impulsive thinking.

Examining the emotional content associated with our automatic thoughts is also essential. Emotions can often cloud our judgment and lead to biased thinking. By acknowledging and understanding the emotions underlying our impulsive thoughts, we can evaluate whether they are appropriate responses to the situation.

Another helpful technique in questioning assumptions is to seek external input. Sharing our automatic thoughts and beliefs with trusted individuals can provide valuable insights and alternative viewpoints. Others may challenge our assumptions by offering different perspectives or additional information we may not have considered.

In addition to external input, we can also engage in self-reflection and introspection. Exploring our cognitive biases, preconceived notions, and personal experiences can help us recognize patterns or tendencies that contribute to impulsive thinking. By gaining self-awareness, we can actively work towards overcoming these biases and developing more rational thought processes.

By engaging in the process of questioning assumptions, we can develop a more nuanced understanding of ourselves and the world around us. We can become more aware of the biases and cognitive distortions that influence our impulsive thinking and take steps to correct them. Through this introspective journey, we can cultivate a more rational and balanced mindset, leading to better decision-making and improved overall well-being.

In the process of challenging impulsive thoughts and reframing automatic reactions, it is crucial to explore alternative perspectives. Our impulsive thoughts are often based on a limited or biased view of a situation, and by seeking alternative interpretations and viewpoints, we can gain a more comprehensive understanding of the situation at hand.

One way to seek alternative perspectives is by considering different viewpoints from others. This involves actively seeking out the opinions and insights of people who may have a different outlook or experience related to the situation. By listening to their perspectives, we can broaden our understanding and challenge preconceived notions or biases that may influence our impulsive thoughts.

Another approach is to engage in self-reflection and introspection. This involves taking a step back from the immediate emotional response triggered by impulsive thoughts and examining the situation from a more objective standpoint. We can uncover different ways of interpreting the situation by questioning our assumptions and considering alternative explanations.

Additionally, it can be helpful to explore different sources of information. In the age of abundant information and diverse media platforms, it is essential to critically evaluate the sources we rely on and seek out alternative viewpoints. By exposing ourselves to various perspectives, we can challenge our biases and gain a more nuanced understanding of the situation.

It is worth noting that seeking alternative perspectives does not mean discarding our beliefs or values. Instead, it is an exercise in expanding our understanding and considering different possibilities. By engaging in this process, we can challenge the rigidity of our impulsive thoughts and develop a more flexible and open-minded approach to interpreting the world around us.

To effectively seek alternative perspectives, it is essential to cultivate curiosity and a willingness to learn. This involves being open to new ideas and actively seeking opportunities to engage with diverse viewpoints. It may also be beneficial to engage in activities promoting empathy and understanding, including reading literature from different cultures or engaging in discussions with others with differing opinions.

Hence, seeking alternative perspectives is valuable in challenging impulsive thoughts and reframing automatic reactions. By exploring different viewpoints, considering alternative interpretations, and actively seeking out diverse perspectives, we can break free from the limitations of our impulsive thoughts and develop a more balanced and nuanced understanding of the world. This process encourages personal growth, critical thinking, and the cultivation of empathy, ultimately leading to more rational and informed decision-making.

Impulsive thoughts often arise from hasty judgments and automatic reactions without careful consideration. To counteract these impulsive tendencies, developing problem-solving strategies that engage critical thinking is crucial. This approach enables us to navigate challenging situations more effectively and make informed decisions.

Problem-solving begins with recognizing that impulsive thoughts may not always lead to the best outcomes. It may involve taking a step back from immediate reactions and actively engaging in a logical thought process. This first requires identifying the specific problem or situation at hand. By clearly defining the issue, we can focus on finding an appropriate solution rather than succumbing to impulsive responses.

Once the problem is defined, it is essential to gather relevant information. This includes considering the context, gathering facts, and seeking different perspectives. Taking the time to gather information allows us to gain a comprehensive understanding of the situation, which can help in generating more thoughtful and well-informed responses. It also helps challenge preconceived notions or biases that may influence impulsive thoughts.

With a solid understanding of the problem and adequate information, critical thinking can be applied to generate potential solutions. This involves thinking creatively and considering multiple alternatives. By brainstorming various possibilities, we can explore a range of perspectives and outcomes. It is important to suspend judgment during this stage and maintain an open mind to all potential solutions, even if they initially seem unconventional or contrary to impulsive thoughts.

Once a list of potential solutions is generated, it is time to evaluate their feasibility and potential consequences. Critical thinking plays a crucial role in this evaluation process. Each solution should be carefully assessed based on its practicality, effectiveness, and potential impact on oneself and others. This evaluation requires a balanced and rational mindset, free from the influence of impulsive thoughts or emotions. It is important to objectively weigh the pros and cons of each solution and consider the long-term implications rather than being swayed by immediate gratification.

After careful evaluation, the most appropriate solution can be selected. This decision should align with one's values, goals, and desired outcomes. It may require compromise or finding a middle ground that satisfies multiple factors. By engaging in critical thinking, we can make well-reasoned decisions less likely to be driven by impulsive thoughts or emotions.

Implementing the chosen solution is the final step in problem-solving. It is essential to develop a plan of action that outlines the necessary steps to be taken and any potential challenges or obstacles that may arise. By having a well-thought-out plan, we can maintain focus and stay on track, reducing the likelihood of succumbing to impulsive thoughts or distractions.

Throughout the problem-solving process, it is essential to remain mindful and self-aware. Regularly reflecting on one's thoughts and actions can help identify recurring impulsive tendencies and provide an opportunity for course correction. By consistently practicing critical thinking and problem-solving strategies, we can gradually overcome impulsive thoughts and develop a more rational and balanced approach to decision-making.

We have embarked on self-discovery and transformation in this empowering chapter on challenging impulsive thoughts. By examining and reframing our automatic reactions, we have gained valuable insights into the nature and impact of impulsive thoughts, paving the way for positive change and personal growth.

Understanding impulsive thoughts has allowed us to unravel the intricate web of influences that shape our lives. We have recognized that impulsive thoughts can significantly affect our well-being and decision-making. Acknowledging their presence and impact, we have taken the first step toward regaining control and living a more intentional and fulfilling life.

Identifying automatic reactions has been a crucial aspect of our journey. We have developed the ability to recognize the triggers that elicit impulsive thoughts, enabling us to break free from their grip. By bringing conscious awareness to our automatic reactions, we have empowered ourselves to respond more deliberately and thoughtfully.

Examining the roots of our impulsive reactions has been a transformative process. We have delved deep into our past experiences, uncovering the underlying causes that fuel impulsive thinking. Through self-reflection and introspection, we have gained valuable insights into the patterns and triggers perpetuating impulsive thoughts, empowering us to challenge and transform them.

Unpacking past experiences has allowed us to understand how they shape our thought patterns. We have embraced the opportunity to heal past wounds, release limiting beliefs, and reframe our perspectives. By revisiting and reframing our past experiences, we have opened the door to personal growth and the possibility of a more positive and empowered future.

The role of emotions in influencing impulsive thoughts has become evident. We have learned to navigate the complex interplay between emotions and impulsive reactions, recognizing that emotions can often cloud our judgment. Through self-awareness and emotional regulation, we have developed the capacity to respond to challenging situations with greater clarity and rationality.

Cognitive restructuring has been a powerful tool in reframing automatic reactions. We have challenged the validity of our impulsive thoughts by examining them logically. By consciously questioning and reshaping our automatic reactions, we have empowered ourselves to adopt more balanced and constructive perspectives

Developing rational thinking has been a cornerstone of our transformation. We have cultivated a mindset rooted in reason and critical thinking, enabling us to approach situations with clarity and objectivity. By embracing rationality, we have unlocked the potential to make more informed decisions and navigate life's challenges with greater wisdom and resilience.

Questioning assumptions has opened the door to expanded possibilities. We have recognized the limitations of our automatic thoughts and beliefs, challenging their validity and exploring alternative perspectives. By fostering a mindset of curiosity and openness, we have embraced the richness of diverse viewpoints, enriching our understanding of the world and ourselves.

Problem-solving strategies have become our allies in overcoming impulsive thoughts. We have harnessed the power of critical thinking to identify creative solutions and navigate obstacles. By employing problem-solving techniques, we have discovered new paths, empowered ourselves to overcome challenges, and embraced a mindset of growth and resilience.

As we conclude this chapter, let us celebrate our progress in challenging our impulsive thoughts. By examining and reframing our automatic reactions, we have reclaimed our agency, fostered personal growth, and cultivated a more intentional and purposeful life. We now possess the tools and insights to navigate life's complexities with greater wisdom, resilience, and positivity. Let us embrace this newfound awareness and continue our journey toward a life filled with mindful choices, empowered decisions, and a sense of inner peace.

MASTER *Your* THOUGHTS

What are thoughts? We all have them and they travel with us as long as we are awake. We cannot run away from them as they live in us. They are fed by what we see, hear, smell, taste, and touch. They are affected by our emotions, depending on what we are thinking. Some say we live in the conscious mind and maintain our livelihood are by opinions, beliefs, perceptions, and ideas gathered from the five senses that are part of the hosting of our well-being.

Thoughts allow us to make sense of the world we live in and what we experience. It allows us to interpret what we see, hear, feels, smell, and taste. Thoughts are modifiable elements that we can change with the information gathered from our attitude, belief, environment, experience, skills, and education. Thoughts are determined through negative and positive thinking patterns which can affect a our mental and emotional well-being.

Negative thoughts can cause and fill our lives with stress, anxiety, justification, and anger which can become overwhelming to bear. Positive thoughts do the opposite, they bring us into the light, instead of darkness, and strengthen our mental and emotional health.

We can be in control of our thoughts and can stop them from taking a detour to the destruction of our lives. When a thought comes to the mind, the mind has the choice to store it in its memory depending on how important it is to the person. If the thoughts are associated with an event of the past that already exists in our memory, then it will stir up an emotion that was registered with that thought. The current thought will become a stimulant that will bring the past thought alive. The memory associated with that emotion will create a world of thoughts that were associated with that past thought creating a web of thoughts, which we find ourselves trapped inside.

As an example, imagine you were walking down the street with your eyes on your cell phone. You were not paying attention to anyone but your phone. In your peripheral vision, your eye picked up a male figure on the other side of the street talking to someone. You are not really paying any attention, except the fact that he is wearing a red t-shirt. You come home to your partner or spouse or some friends or family member. It's around dinner time, and usually every day there is a routine when you come home. You may join your partner, friends, or family to watch a show before dinner or relax with a snack. Most of the time you will all cook together or decide on eating out or ordering in. Your usual routine would be to go to the kitchen to see if food is made and grab a snack. Today was one of those days you went to the kitchen expecting snacks or a meal. But you notice there is dirty glass in the sink and a few dirty pots and pans on the stove. This was not unusual, however, a wave of anger rose from the inside and you took the dirty glass and smash it on the floor saying "you have been home all day, why is there nothing to eat and dirty dishes in the kitchen?" Although the routine was not abnormal, there was a burst of anger which was unexpected.

As a psychological assessment is completed, the person getting angry recall his day and his journey home. The only unusual thing that happened that day was man on the opposite side of the road wearing a red t-shirt. What is unusual about this is the fact that when you were about six years old, you were sexually abused by an older person wearing a red t-shirt that looks similar to what the man was wearing. The figure of the person looked the same, yet you did not pay any attention to the man with the red t-shirt. A memory card was triggered with an underlining unresolved issue. As the memory card got triggered, anger was released affecting your mental and psychological well-being. In simple words, we need to resolve unresolved issues, as they can be triggered anytime anywhere like a time bomb as they are retained in mind.

All thoughts revolve around one major thought and are created and developed from the amount of attention we give them. A single thought can expand to multiple thoughts if we don't contain it. Thoughts feed from any of our sensory nerves, especially what we hear and what we see. They get energy from whatever is connected to our five senses that have relevance to our thoughts. The dominant thought likes to be the center of attention which will justify every idea that comes to the mind to stay in control and be fed.

We all make decisions consciously or subconsciously without thinking. We all have impulsive reactions when provoked, and depending on the topic, we can even become defensive and rude. We need to give ourselves time to process a thought before impulsively answering, especially when the thought is a trigger to us. We all have regrets for things we say, mistakes we wish never happened, and the flaws and weaknesses that we present. Although it is difficult to admit it, we are not perfect. Our imperfections are seen through our thought processes and how we vocalize issues and solutions. When we are able to process any friction or give ourselves time to ponder what we collide with, we will have a better resolution. We will have less stress while cleaning up the mess we created when we allow our minds to think about what we heard and dissect it before concluding how we feel.

Individuals struggling with their mental health conditions, addictions, and psychological traumas carries multiple thoughts in their mind. Those with addiction issues think of all the reasons to justify their use with the main thought "this will be the last time." Those with anxiety may struggle from a thought that is triggered by an abusive relationship or a traumatic event. Those with psychosis could have a thought stuck in their mind, and feel pressured to act on the thought, especially if it is being driven by command hallucinations.

Words we hear can trigger an unfavorable memory created in the past. Words have a tendency to look for other words to form a sentence, particularly negative words. Our brain will search for every word that connects to statements or situations and formulate a sentence. When we have unresolved situations, our brain looks for a vocabulary of words to express feelings. When we recondition the mind, we gain the power to flush out negative words and experiences, and replace them with positivity. Individuals struggling with depression or a mood disorder only perceive darkness, and as a result, develop a pessimistic approach which leads to hopelessness and suicidal thoughts. When a person is able to change their thought process and implement positive words, they can turn on the 'optimism' switch in the mind. Nevertheless, every dark room has a light switch, we just need to find it.

Everyone has the power to stop negative thinking from learned therapies. The mind needs to be distracted, even for thirty seconds. For example, during your work hours, you may develop a need to use the washroom and on your way to the washroom, you may meet someone. You spend about ten minutes talking to them about something and your mind switches the thought of the need to use the washroom to another topic. You may not end up going to the washroom after that conversation as the mind may forget where you were going. However, in a short while, your thought of wanting to go to the washroom will return.

Another example would be driving down the street and smelling food. Although you may have had a meal earlier, the smell of food triggers the brain. Same as seeing someone eat ice cream, someone with a coffee or a burger. Once our sensory nerves are triggered, we develop urges or cravings. Unhealthy urges and cravings can lead to bigger issues. That's why we need to develop a habit of being able to distract our thoughts even for thirty seconds if we want to rewire the brain. This small habit of processing our thoughts will make a huge difference in our lives.

We could be watching a television commercial advertising a coconut cream pie or fried chicken and suddenly we develop urges or cravings desiring it and want it right away. Just like watching an advertisement for cars, trucks, clothes, and so on. If we have a buying habit, we will make an online purchase, or head down to the store to satisfy the craving. Several people purchase clothes from window shopping, or what they see others wearing, especially if it is of a popular brand or worn by someone who is a celebrity.

Thoughts are more prominent in the mind just before falling asleep. And, depending on the nature of the thoughts, we could be stuck with a thought or developed racing thoughts. Thoughts will eventually become like a movie playing in the mind, especially if they are thoughts accumulated during the day by a disagreement or a regret. We have to learn how to manipulate thoughts, creating distractions or diversion thoughts which this workbook will teach.

Thoughts can affect your eating habits, your sleeping patterns, concentration, memory, and other daily functions. They can spiral down into depression and anxiety. We all tend to look for coping strategies that will work quickly, which usually are negative. Gambling, alcohol, street drugs, misuse of prescription medications, and self-harm are usually the choices for a quick fix. But this workbook teaches other ways that are positive and healthy. Moreover, you will also learn how to take advantage of your disadvantage and implement strategies that help you to gain control of your thoughts, instead of your thoughts leading you.

Taking control of the thought is the first step to strengthening the mind and re-training your thinking patterns. Positive thinking is the second step to reconditioning the mind and becoming optimistic even in the storms of life. Re-phrasing what you think or restructuring your thoughts is the third step to bring healing to your emotional life. And, living for what you assume to be fruitful is the fourth step to carry you to be a master over your thoughts.

We need to master our thoughts. We need to remind ourselves that masters are not born; they are made. We need to look at ways to become a master over our thoughts in order to conquer our addictions, anxieties, and depression. Master s use their weakness as strengths, they use their regrets, mistakes, and hurts as fertilizer to fertilize their future, they push hard to overcome their weakness, they strive to win and are not easily distracted, and they are competitive and do not give room for failure. We need to strive towards being a master over our thoughts if we want to move out of the pit of feeling low and depressed. We must see the light at the end of the tunnel, the light switch on the wall of a dark room. We must see the anchor that will sustain us from drifting in the sea of life. We must see the bigger picture of our lives, where we want to be, where we can be, and what would it take to get there.

Master s look at the worse situation that could have happened and remind themselves that there are worse situations than theirs. They look at where they are in life and where they would want to be. They tell themselves exactly what they want to hear. They have mastered the concept of enjoying who they are. They feel comfortable dating themselves and falling in love with who they see in the mirror. They don't rely on others to add value and worth to their lives, nor are they co-dependent on others. Master s are confident that life has much to offer if they take the necessary steps to reach their goals.

We are all masters if we chose. It means we need to practice gaining control, train ourselves to be the best, think positively, and be optimistic about life. When a thought comes that has no bearing of fruitfulness, we should not waste time entertaining them. Some of us may have thoughts including "I feel like a failure," "nobody understands me," and "what's the purpose of my life anyway." We need to recondition the mind with "I am not a failure," "I don't need others to understand me," "My life has purpose and value" and "I have a bright future waiting for me to discover with family and friends" "I love the gift of life and admire the person I see in the mirror." We flush our minds with positive affirmations and the tools in this book will help with distractions and diversions to see the value and worth we carry as a person.

Mastering our thoughts does not mean that we will have no more negative thoughts. We will be surprised to know negative thoughts are a normal part of our thinking process and even from birth, our brain is hardwired to be more negative as we develop picking up information like a sponge from all those around us. As we grow up, whatever have tainted the mind, control our thinking and regulates our thoughts. The problem that arise when we failed to control our negative thoughts, is the fact that they consume us mentally, emotionally and psychologically. Our lives become miserable, and we become victim to a number of mental disorders.

Not all mental or psychological issues originates from negative thinking, but they can stem from them. Negative thoughts can be responsible for how we process what we feel without exploring options to be in control. We need to eradicate all negative thinking before the thoughts consumes us, leaving us bitter, angry, frustrated, and miserable with ourselves.

It can be a challenge to stay positive when life is full of problems that are overwhelming and stress related. differentiate between negative thinking and worries that leads to stress. We need to program ourselves that negativity will lead us to depressive symptoms and create lack of motivation. It will affect how we function on a day-to-day level at the workplace, with the family, at home and our own personal life. We will not feel like we could achieve anything and give up without even trying. We will be sad, angry, and exhausted with does not work well together. We will see the entire world around us being the problem than seeing that changes need to come from in the inside out. Some of us may get sick from allowing negativity to percolate like coffee. We must learn to identify negative thoughts and work towards conditioning the mind to stay positive, regardless of life's situation. There is always light at the end of the tunnel, be the first to see it.

With a positive outlook in mind, we can gain determination, confidence, and willpower to achieve desired results. Whereas with a negative outlook, even the smallest task seems difficult and a challenge for us to pursue.

Many of us are often afraid of the future developing anxiety. We need to master the way we think to be in control of not allowing unnecessary thoughts to fill our mind. We are often afraid of the unknown and unsure of what the future holds for us. This often leads to failure in the mind when there is no motivation to pursue goals. No matter how we look at it, worrying about the future is a waste of time and energy, and it leads to negative thinking. The key to getting rid of these negative thoughts is to acknowledge that there is a limitation as to what we can do and what we cannot do. The ultimate goal is to focus on taking baby steps and not setting goals that we are unable to meet. This will help avoid unnecessary disappointments.

We all make mistakes from time to time, as we are not perfect. We all have flaws and does things that we have regrets. We all say things we are ashamed of, but people with a negative mindset tend to focus more on past mistakes, flaws, failures and regrets than others. We have to remind ourselves that we are not perfect and that's okay. When we acknowledge that we have flaws and failures and regrets we wish we can change, we need to work on avoiding making the same mistakes twice. We want to focus on staying positive and not allowing our minds to go down the rabbit hole where we isolate ourselves from others. We cannot change the past, but we can change the future.

We all have responsibilities in life like everyone else, especially financially. And, in order to grow up and mature we need to take on the responsibility of being financially stable. There are times when things can go against our financial plans and expectations, creating worry and fear. We have to remind ourselves there are no shortcuts to life. If we don't work hard, we will never have enough money to survive without living from paycheck to paycheck. We may suffer financial instability when we find it difficult to settle at a job or chose a career path, when there is spending habit, we find difficult to control, lack of resources, and lack of motivation to go back to school and educate ourselves with a proper education. A lack of financial stability brings negative thinking to the mind as some of us may not be able to past the thought we need to change and not the system. If we believe we can work less and gain more money, we need a plan. We believe in the get rich quick scheme we will soon learn it does not work. If we believe we have a product to see or go on self-employed we need to make sure we understand it may take some time before the business blossom. We need to convince the mind that we have a blueprint, a plan for our future to avoid financial instability.

We should not allow our confidence level to speak for us and make unwise decisions. Usually lack of confidence can manifest itself in control, frustration and anger. We may think we are never good enough; we cannot do what we put our minds to do, there are more qualities than us and we love hope. We could be an introvert or extrovert we all can struggle with confidence issues, which leads to negative thinking. We have to mind ourselves that confidence can only grow when we lead the principles of developing our skills, knowledge and experience. The more we practice our growing in our areas of weaknesses, the more our confidence level will increase. Sometimes we may need to bluff our way in a situation for confidence to manifest itself. You assume you don't have the skills to do the job. You cannot fulfill your potential. Our lack of confidence can also be responsible for low self-esteem which leads to negative thinking.

Thinking and worrying about something is normal but the real problem arises when this type of thinking becomes continuous. So many of us can be over thinkers, where we may have a bad experience or someone may have said something to us and we hold on to that thought over and over again. We have to replace negative thoughts with someone positive. We have to remind ourselves that we cannot change a person or what they think, but we can change how we accommodate them. We have to avoid our minds from thoughts that are destructive as the thoughts will become our impulsive thoughts which will be a challenge to break. Overthinking can result from regrets and wrong choices we made in the past regarding education, career, employment, family dynamics, relationships, marriages, social lifestyles, spirituality, financial and other psychosocial issues. Moreover, overthinking is believed to be the primary cause of negative thinking resulting in severe mental problems including depression, anxiety and psychosis. Overthinking can affect our psychological well-being leading to negative thinking and unrealistic expectations.

We all can set unrealistic expectations for ourselves, relationships, family and friends, parenting, career and employment, education, and budgeting. We need to be realistic when we set a goals for our lives. We need to be realistic otherwise we will become more frustration which leads to negative thinking. Several of us who set unrealistic or unachievable goals find ourselves through processing our thoughts to engage in negative thinking. We want to avoid losing self-confidence and motivation to become an achiever. We need to focus on that which we know is our destiny for our lives and avoid blaming others for our wrong choices or bad decision we make.

It is very easy to blame ourselves or others when negative things occurs, like spending money and not having enough left over to pay the bills, getting involved in a automobile accident, losing a love one from an unexpected incident. Very often when something negative happens in our lives we blame ourselves or others instead of accepting the mistake and moving forward. We cannot replace a jar when it falls to the ground and break, so why blame. Like the old saying "why cry over spilled milk." We need to work on resolutions, otherwise we get the blaming concepts to manifest itself through negative thinking which is manifested through unhealthy choices.

Living a unhealthy lifestyle is really a choice, even though there would not be a lot of people who would not agree. We all love to eat from time to time, and in our western culture we have so many fast food that makes it easy accessible for buy. Some of us may eat out of convenience when we are hungry and others out of cravings. As much as we can manage our intake of illicit drugs, alcohol, and negativity from others we could also manage unhealthy living. Unhealthy living is not just wrong choices of food intake, it is the lifestyle we choose to live. It may mean avoiding exercising, socializing, developing spirituality, positive thinking, and the places and things that we are addicted to. Anything we do that will harm ourselves is considered unhealthy. We need to take pride in who we are and the value and worth we carry as a person. Unhealthy living brings regrets which creates negative thinking.

Our emotions and thoughts can have a significant impact on our physical health and how we function as a person. Living in freedom where we avoid judge it ourselves and others can relief a lot of unnecessary weight on our shoulders. Negative thinking builds stress and other psychological issues that can weigh us down. It can drain us emotionally where we are like a well without the flow of water. We feel exhausted and find it difficult to relax or even have fun with others. Furthermore, negative thoughts can influence our relationships, marriages, academic performance, work life, and socializing. They also affects our path to a happy and successful life. Negative thinking affects our psychological well-being.

Fortunately, there are many scientifically proven ways that provide an effective solution to negative thinking which are evidence-based. To live a happy and well-balanced life we have to learn how to dance to the sounds of life. We need to learn how to recondition the mind and restructure our thinking. We need to flush out the negativity to positivity. There are many tips to do so, however we need to become aware of the change we need to make otherwise it will not happen. We need to implement changes that will benefit our mental and spiritual wellbeing. We should learn how to catch ourselves and create new neuropathways that are of a positive nature. It will not be an easy task, but it will be worth it at the end, when others compliment us of the changes they see. When we learn to live happy, calm and peaceful internally, it will manifest itself externally.

We all to learn the healthy stimulants is good for the brain. A change of environment can do this for us. We have to know that it is okay to develop a distance between toxic people and still maintain a relationship with them. Our minds are fed like our stomach with the environment we live in. It can be what goes on at work, social media we view, the music we listen to, the movies we watch, the news, who we have as role models or blueprints in our lives, and those who influence us. It's like the dog who had several pops. The dog was hit by a car which left her with a broken leg. She was not helped and walked with a limp. All her puppies walked with a limp as they thought their mother's way of walking was the right way.

Another healthy stimulant is physical activity which helps develop dopamine's and serotonins. Going for walks, the gym, exercising, excursions, tours, getting involved in a sport, running, bird watching, people watching, window shopping, photography, scrapbooking etc. Anything that involves physical activity will stimulate the brain through the five sensory nerves, releasing dopamine's and serotonins. This is our stress relievers that will help maintain happiness. We need to incorporate at lease thirty minutes a day to something that can involve physical activity, it will help with our anxiety level.

Talk therapy has always been part of human nature. When we talk to someone, we can feel like a weight has left us. It is difficult to find trustworthy people, hence it is important to find therapist. So many of us struggle to talk about our concerns, our feelings and things that bothers us. Yet talking to someone has helped millions of people around the world. People pay a lot of money to share their thoughts with professionals, where they can empty their mind and find ways to fill it with healthy thoughts. There are certain people who will come across your life where you can develop a trust to share certain things that bothers you. Nothing is wrong in getting a second opinion. Sometimes our pride prevents us from talking to others as we believe we have the answer or we know it all. We could never know it all; we could never have the answers to all of the struggles we go through and burying our feelings under the rug will cause us to stumble and fall flat on our faces. We burn a lot of bridges when we keep everything inside and live a superficial shallow life. Directly and indirectly things that bothers us will only exacerbates if we keep it inside our mind. We will overthink or we will bury them which will be triggered by others with similar incidents or encounters. Some religious group finds it easy to talk to someone and share their heart, some talk to God, some talk to a friend, some a therapist and others themselves. We need to talk to someone about deep issues or incidents that has occurred to avoid bigger problems as we age.

Another important healthy stimulant is learning to volunteer our time in humanitarian aid. It is important to do some form of humanitarian work. People who help others develop a happiness internally with words that they themselves cannot explain. Most hospitals, libraries, shelters, foodbanks, churches, orphanages, and supporting the less fortunate started with volunteers. Life is about giving, what can we do for others instead of what we can get from others. When we do something for others, we will soon realize that there are others in worse cases than us. Sometimes we may believe that our issues of life is worse and no one can ever understand, until we start helping others. Feeding the poor, help build a house in a third world country, volunteer at a shelter, give donations to the less fortunate, visit an orphanage, go on a mission trip somewhere and you will be in awe of the problems people deal with. We would appreciate what we have and who we are very quickly.

Learn to be grateful for everything in life, the little things and the big things. The fact that we have life, treat it like there is no tomorrow. Treat others with respect and dignity like today is the last day you will see them. Developing gratitude and showing how grateful you are will open doors to people's hearts, including yours. Gratefulness keeps us humble and focused on being positive. It's difficult to be grateful and be negative. When we are fighting negativity, it's easy to forget all the positive things in our lives, making it a challenge to be grateful.

Keeping a journal of our feelings and emotions is a good way to empty the mind. We all should be keeping a log of our day on a journal; this will help with getting rid of negative thoughts. We need to write down our feelings and emotions and how others have impacted our lives in a positive way. Taking ten to fifteen minutes a day will be like medicine to the soul. Keeping a log will show our progress and will help with a determination of having a healthy thought process. We would want to generate more positive thoughts than negative thoughts on our notebook, therefore we will become more mindful on controlling what we think.

Mindfulness techniques, meditation, deep breathing, relaxation exercises, and various other self-awareness methods help us to control our emotional reactions to situations. We need to learn how to smell the imaginary rose and blow out the imaginary candle when overwhelmed and is in a anxious mode. They allow our minds to take over our thought processes. Practicing mindfulness contribute to the ability to use our thoughts more adaptively with fewer negative thoughts. There are a lot of teaching on mindfulness, meditation, diaphragmic breathing and other self-awareness methods that helps reduce negative thinking.

We need to identify our thoughts in order to rule them out. When we identify our thoughts and note down, we can evaluate their cause for floating around our minds. As we watch our thoughts and identify them, we will be able to regulate them and replace them with positive thoughts. Although it is not as simple to replace negative thoughts with positive thoughts, identifying the cause of negative thoughts will get us to the root. And, when we can remove the negative roots and replant positive ones, we can have healthy thoughts. We will need to work on willpower, self-control, and mindfulness techniques to remain calm when we feel triggered with this process. With that being said, some thoughts are activated because we have not put closure to an incident.

It is important to bring closure to incidents or situations that creates negative thinking. There are many ways to bring closure to the past that is affecting the future. We need to replace the negative memory card with positive memory card. We may need to write down our past on paper and burn it with a celebrate so the brain identifies an ending to the past as a celebration. We would draw the past in an image form in the mind and place them in a mirror, breaking them to pieces where they no longer exist as a whole in image in the mind, replacing the pieces with a new image in the mind. We could put the past in a bottle and see it float away from you. There are lots of closure suggestions that can be implemented to rid of the negative thinking. When we chose to do so, we will create new habits that will be healthy, protecting our minds from the battle is goes through from thinking negatively.

New habits are like learning a language or writing with the less dominant hand. It takes time but has positive results at the end. Instead of trying to overcome negative thought patterns, try to replace them with new habits. We need to turn our attention from harmful thinking to a healthy lifestyle that we can enjoy. Begin with something simple, easy, and most importantly, something you really enjoy that will take your mind off negative thoughts.

CONCLUSION

In conclusion, mastering your thoughts was a profound journey of self-discovery and empowerment. Throughout this booklet, we've explored the intricate terrain of the human mind, shedding light on the various types of thoughts that influence our emotions, behaviours, and overall well-being. By understanding and mastering our thoughts, we unlocked the key to inner peace, resilience, and a greater sense of control over our lives.

We began with examining self-destructive thoughts, those insidious weeds that infiltrate the garden of our minds, choking out the flowers of positivity and growth. We learned that self-destructive thoughts often stem from feelings of unworthiness, fear, or past traumas. However, through practices such as self-compassion, therapy, and mindfulness, we can challenge negative beliefs and nurture a mindset of self-love and acceptance.

Next, we explored the realm of intrusive thoughts, those unwanted guests that invade our mental space without invitation. We discovered that everyone experiences intrusive thoughts to some degree, but they can become particularly distressing when they occur with frequency or intensity. Yet, by practicing mindfulness, grounding techniques, and cognitive-behavioral therapy (CBT), we can learn to observe intrusive thoughts without judgment and let them pass like clouds in the sky.

Finally, we reviewed the realm of impulsive thoughts, those wild horses that gallop through our minds, urging us to act on impulse without consideration of the consequences. We recognized that impulsive thoughts often arise in moments of stress, boredom, or emotional intensity. However, by developing greater self-awareness and impulse control, we can interrupt the automatic cycle of impulsivity and make more deliberate choices.

Throughout this journey, we've uncovered practical strategies and exercises to help us cultivate mental clarity, inner peace, and emotional well-being. Whether it's journaling, meditation, or self-reflection, each tool serves as a beacon of light guiding us towards a more empowered mindset.

As we bid farewell to this booklet, let us remember that mastering our thoughts is not a destination but a lifelong practice. It requires dedication, patience, and a willingness to confront our inner demons head-on. Yet, the rewards are immeasurable. By mastering our thoughts, we unlock the transformative power of our minds and create a life filled with purpose, joy, and fulfillment.

So, let us embrace this journey with open hearts and open minds. Let us continue to challenge negative beliefs, reframe distorted thinking, and cultivate a greater sense of self-awareness and compassion. For in doing so, we not only master our thoughts but also unlock the limitless potential within ourselves.